MAJOR BATTLES IN US HISTORY

THE BATTLES OF LEXINGTON AND CONCORD

START OF THE AMERICAN REVOLUTION

by Wil Mara

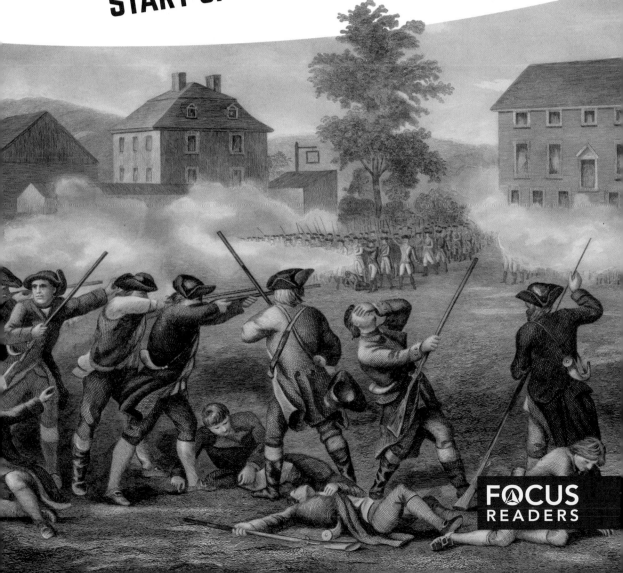

FOCUS
READERS

North Star
EDITIONS

WWW.NORTHSTAREDITIONS.COM

Produced for North Star Editions by Red Line Editorial.

Photographs ©: Library of Congress, cover, 1; Red Line Editorial, 5, 21; North Wind Picture Archives, 6–7, 9, 10–11, 14, 16, 18–19, 22, 25; FineArt/Alamy, 26–27

Content Consultant: Walter R. Borneman, author of *American Spring: Lexington, Concord, and the Road to Revolution*

ISBN
978-1-63517-023-8 (hardcover)
978-1-63517-079-5 (paperback)
978-1-63517-183-9 (ebook pdf)
978-1-63517-133-4 (hosted ebook)

Library of Congress Control Number: 2016951031

Printed in the United States of America
Mankato, MN
November, 2016

ABOUT THE AUTHOR

Wil Mara is the author of more than 200 books, many of which are educational titles for young readers.

TABLE OF CONTENTS

1763: Great Britain and France agree to end the French and Indian War.

1765: British leaders tax American colonists to help pay for the war's expenses. American colonists are outraged.

1768: British troops go to Boston, Massachusetts, to stop a potential public uprising.

1773: To protest new taxes, including a tax on tea, a group of colonists destroys a shipment of British tea.

1775: Confrontations between colonists and British soldiers occur at Lexington and Concord, launching the American Revolution.

1776: The Second Continental Congress drafts and signs the Declaration of Independence.

1783: Great Britain surrenders to the colonists, ending the American Revolution.

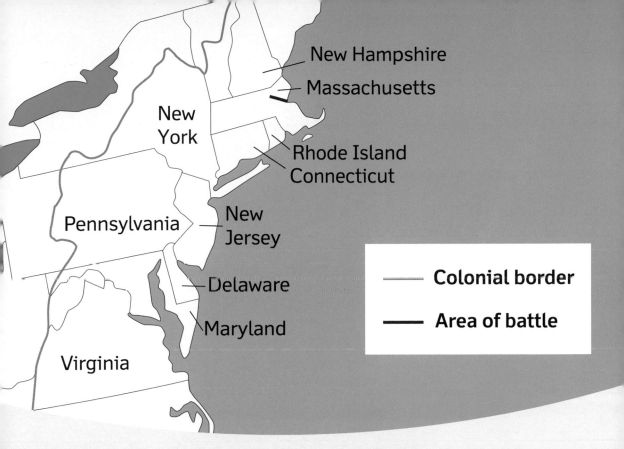

New Hampshire
Massachusetts
New York
Rhode Island
Connecticut
Pennsylvania
New Jersey
Delaware
Maryland
Virginia

———— Colonial border

—— Area of battle

BATTLES OF LEXINGTON AND CONCORD

	BRITISH	AMERICAN COLONISTS
Killed	73	49
Wounded	174	39
Missing	26	5

CHAPTER 1

THE BATTLE OF LEXINGTON

At 5:00 a.m. on April 19, 1775, approximately 700 British soldiers marched into Lexington, Massachusetts. The soldiers wore bright-red uniforms and marched in a long column. Three officers led the way on horseback. The soldiers were on their way to Concord, Massachusetts.

British soldiers were known as Redcoats, or Regulars.

The British controlled all 13 of the American **colonies**. But the British had heard that an American **militia** might rise up against British rule. The militia was hiding military supplies in Concord. British soldiers were on their way to destroy these supplies.

The soldiers marched into the center of Lexington. There, across a small field, nearly 80 armed colonists stood in a line. A British officer shouted at the militiamen, telling them to lay down their weapons and return to their homes. Suddenly, a gunshot rang out. People on both sides panicked. Amid the confusion, British soldiers fired on the colonists.

The leader of the Lexington militia told his men to return to their homes, but a gunshot caused the battle to erupt.

Most of the colonists ran for their lives, but a few returned fire. The British ran forward with their **bayonets** out. By the time the battle was over, eight colonists had received wounds that would take their lives.

CHAPTER 2

TROUBLE IN THE COLONIES

Tensions between American colonists and the British government had been growing long before April 1775. In the early 1750s, most colonists were proud to be under British rule. When a war broke out between Great Britain and France in 1754, colonists were ready to fight for the British cause.

Colonial soldiers led by George Washington (top) fought for the British in the mid-1700s.

11

By the war's end, British forces, including colonial soldiers, had driven French troops out of North America. But Great Britain had spent lots of money on the war. To raise more money, Great Britain's leaders decided to **tax** American colonists. The Stamp Act of 1765 placed a tax on paper goods such as newspapers, legal documents, and playing cards. Taxes such as these greatly upset colonists. The colonists also felt they did not have a way to voice their concerns in the British government.

The British government added more taxes. In 1767, the Townshend Acts taxed items such as paint, glass, lead, and British tea. The taxes led some colonists to respond with violence. On December 16, 1773, a group of colonists boarded three ships in Boston, Massachusetts. They destroyed an entire shipment of British tea.

TAXES IN THE COLONIES

April 5, 1764:
Sugar Act enforces a tax on sugar and molasses. The act also cuts the supply of non-British sources of these items.

May 15, 1765:
Quartering Act requires colonists to pay for British soldiers' supplies and housing in the colonies.

March 18, 1766:
British Parliament issues the Declaratory Act, repealing the Stamp Act but upholding Britain's right to tax colonists.

March 22, 1765:
Stamp Act creates taxes on paper goods and requires colonists to print on paper produced in Great Britain.

October 1765:
Colonial leaders gather and declare the Stamp Act unconstitutional.

June 29, 1767:
Townshend Acts tax paper, tea, glass, and other items to pay for administrative duties associated with running the colonies.

Colonists dressed as American Indians threw boxes of tea overboard during the Boston Tea Party.

They dumped much of it overboard. The event was called the Boston Tea Party.

The British government reacted by creating a new set of laws colonists called the Intolerable Acts. The laws reinforced British control over the colonies.

The laws also weakened the colonial government in Massachusetts. Despite the laws, colonists in Massachusetts formed the Massachusetts Provincial Congress. This government became a statement of independence for the colonists. British leaders were increasingly worried the colonists might rebel. So the British government instructed General Thomas Gage to start disarming colonial militias. Gage was also told to arrest Samuel Adams and John Hancock. These men were leaders of a group called the Sons of Liberty. The Sons of Liberty felt the colonists should break free from British rule.

Members of the Sons of Liberty met in secret to plan ways to rebel against British rule.

Joseph Warren was another leader of the Sons of Liberty. He had spies among the British military who learned of Gage's orders. Warren sent fellow **revolutionary** Paul Revere to Concord on April 8, 1775.

Revere warned Concord's leaders that the British were planning to march to the town and seize the militia's supplies. Revere's message allowed colonists to spread the supplies into homes and shops in nearby towns.

On the evening of April 18, 1775, Warren received word that British troops were assembling in Boston. They were headed across the Charles River, toward Lexington. It was the moment the Sons of Liberty had been waiting for. Warren needed to make sure the militias were ready to stand their ground.

CHAPTER 3

THE SHOT HEARD ROUND THE WORLD

As British soldiers prepared to cross the Charles River, Gage tried to stop all colonists from leaving Boston. He hoped word would not spread that British troops were getting ready to march. Unknown to Gage, William Dawes and Paul Revere of the Sons of Liberty were already riding to Lexington on horseback.

Paul Revere rode to Lexington, alerting colonists along the way the British were leaving Boston.

Dawes and Revere took different routes so that if one of the men was captured, the other might still raise the alarm. Both riders reached Lexington. They warned Hancock and Adams that the British were on their way. From Lexington, more riders went out to gather militiamen from the surrounding areas. Revere and Dawes continued toward Concord. On the way, they were joined by a young doctor named Samuel Prescott. A little after 1:00 a.m., the three came across a British **patrol**. Only Prescott escaped and continued to Concord.

After the early morning battle in Lexington, the British soldiers marched to

NIGHTTIME RIDERS

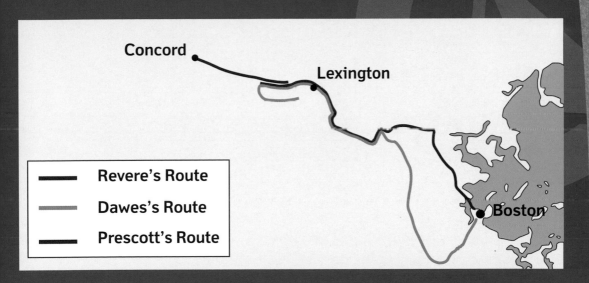

Concord
Lexington
Boston

Revere's Route
Dawes's Route
Prescott's Route

Concord. Once they arrived, the soldiers searched all the properties in which they believed supplies were hidden. Many of the supplies had already been moved, so the soldiers did not find much. But they destroyed the supplies they did find.

Militiamen forced British soldiers to retreat from the North Bridge in Concord.

Meanwhile, a small group of British soldiers had gathered around a narrow bridge that spanned the Concord River.

More than 400 militiamen approached the bridge. As each side faced the other across the river, they readied their weapons.

No one gave the order to fire. But one of the British soldiers let off a single shot. Then there was another and another. Two militiamen were killed. The colonists fired back. Knowing they were outnumbered, the British fled. Some British soldiers continued to search for military supplies. But eventually all British troops began marching back to Boston.

Along the road, militiamen gathered in wooded hills and along high ridges. They fired down on the British soldiers.

The British fired back, but they were in a bad position to fight and were quickly running out of **ammunition**. The weary British soldiers received help at Lexington. There, more than 1,000 British soldiers joined the battle.

The British took a break to rest and eat. At 3:30 p.m., they set off for Boston. More colonial soldiers had arrived by this time, and they continued to attack the British soldiers along the road to Boston. As the British entered the town of Menotomy, Massachusetts, the fighting became more vicious. Frustrated British soldiers attacked townspeople who were not involved in the battle.

Colonists hid behind hilltops and trees as they attacked the retreating British troops.

Word spread of the violence against **civilians**. By the time the British reached Charlestown, which lay across the Charles River from Boston, thousands of militiamen had gathered in the area. By the following morning, Boston was surrounded by colonial troops.

CHAPTER 4

THE BEGINNING OF INDEPENDENCE

The battles at Lexington and Concord forever changed the relationship between American colonists and the British government. The British were shocked by the defeat. Their military was one of the finest in the world. In addition, the British viewed colonial militias as disorganized and undertrained.

The loss to the American revolutionaries was an embarrassment for British general Thomas Gage.

The victory gave colonists confidence. It proved the British could be defeated. Many people changed their minds about seeking American independence. Some had not been sure if the colonists should try to break free of British rule. But when they learned of the brutal manner in which British troops gunned down civilians, they decided independence was necessary.

In May 1775, **representatives** from the 13 American colonies met in Pennsylvania at a meeting known as the Second Continental Congress. At the meeting, the representatives decided to create a shared army among the colonies.

The actions of the Second Continental Congress marked the formal start of the American Revolution. But many historians consider the battles at Lexington and Concord to be the war's true starting point.

WAR BY THE NUMBERS

2.5 MILLION
people lived in the colonies, compared to 8 million in Great Britain.

231,000
Americans served in the Continental Army during the American Revolution.

40,000
soldiers from both sides fought at the war's largest battle, the battle of Long Island.

24,000
British soldiers died, went missing, or were captured during the war.

6,800
Americans were killed in battle, with another 17,000 dying from disease.

101
months after fighting broke out at Lexington and Concord, the war was over.

FOCUS ON
THE BATTLES OF LEXINGTON AND CONCORD

Write your answers on a separate piece of paper.

1. Summarize why the colonists wanted independence.

2. Why do you think the first shot fired at the battle of Concord is known as the Shot Heard round the World?

3. Which nighttime rider made it to Concord?

   A. Paul Revere
   B. Samuel Prescott
   C. William Dawes

4. Which negative outcome may have occurred if the colonists did not learn of Gage's plan?

   A. The British may have successfully taken the militia's supplies.
   B. The British may have fared better at the battles of Lexington and Concord.
   C. The British may have arrested Paul Revere.

Answer key on page 32.

GLOSSARY

ammunition
Objects that are shot from weapons.

bayonets
Long knives attached to the ends of rifles.

civilians
People who are not in the military.

colonies
Areas controlled by a country that is far away.

militia
A group of citizens organized for military service.

patrol
A soldier or group of soldiers sent out to inspect an area.

representatives
People chosen to speak on behalf of a group.

revolutionary
A person who supports extreme changes in the government.

tax
To charge a fee in addition to the normal cost of an item or service.

TO LEARN MORE

BOOKS

Archer, Jules. *They Made a Revolution: The Sons and Daughters of the American Revolution.* New York: Sky Pony, 2016.

Krull, Kathleen. *What Was the Boston Tea Party?* New York: Grosset & Dunlap, 2016.

Murray, Stuart. *American Revolution.* New York: DK, 2015.

NOTE TO EDUCATORS

Visit **www.focusreaders.com** to find lesson plans, activities, links, and other resources related to this title.

INDEX

Answer Key: **1.** Answers will vary; **2.** Answers will vary; **3.** B; **4.** A